Why Geese Honk

Randy Gadient

ISBN-10: 1499205163
ISBN-13: 978-1499205169

To my birds of a feather…

Contents

Introduction

We can learn a lot from geese.

Geese are incredible birds. Every year, geese accomplish something amazing - they travel half-way across the world. When geese fly together, they can fly almost twice as far as when they fly alone. It's natural. Success in life is natural.

This book is not just about geese.
This book is about life.
This book will ask more questions than it answers.
The answers are up to you.

Whatever your situation is in life, I hope that this book is a source of encouragement for you.

I hope that somewhere between its ten simple chapters this book helps you to see something new.

After all, there is a lot of beauty in nature – you just need to see it...

Chapter 1
Why Geese Honk

Have you ever wondered why geese honk? All birds make noise of some form, but geese are different, aren't they? Geese honk. They also fly amazing distances every year – literally thousands of miles in beautiful formation, choosing where they want to be, and supporting each other throughout life's journey. Wouldn't it be wonderful if our lives were like that?

Geese accomplish something amazing every single year of their lives. Geese don't spend years or even months of their lives planning a journey across the continent, collecting copious information on what lies ahead, carefully considering the risks and benefits of adventure, and then meticulously training for what must be an incredibly taxing journey before they take the huge leap of faith and start that journey.

No – they just do it – and they do it every year. It's *natural* for them. Quite simply, geese find like-minded birds, get into formation, stick their neck out, and fly, honking the whole way. Wouldn't it be wonderful if we accomplished something amazing every single year?

What if we knew exactly what we needed right now to achieve something incredible this year? What if we could naturally make our wonderful future happen? How good would that be?

Imagine for a moment that you are a goose halfway along this incredible annual journey across the world. You have been flying for hours, and now you are in the thick of a threatening storm; the wind is contesting every inch of progress, rain is beating down on your entire body, and each drop of icy rain reminds you of the insufferable cold you are in. To make matters worse, every muscle in your body is in pure agony from the countless hours of continuous flight that you've been in the air. Every physical fiber of your being wants to give up. But you don't.

There are only two things stopping you.

First, you look around you, and the other geese with you are in the exact same condition – they've been flying for hours and hours, and they are still going – they have to keep going. You realise that you are a part of something special – you are surrounded by wonderful creatures that you would rather endure the hardship with than leave the hardship without.

Second, one of them starts honking. Pretty soon, all of them are…

When geese honk, they encourage each other. Encouragement is a miraculous gift – it doesn't cost anything to encourage someone, and it always has a return - always. Positive expression creates a positive future.

Your words create your reality.

We are all on life's journey. We all need encouragement. Geese encourage each other all the time, and just look at what they can do. How often do you encourage others?

Let's learn from geese. Let's be like geese. Say something encouraging to the next person you happen to see. Form a new habit, and encourage others around you as often as you can. You will soon learn one of nature's best kept secrets:

We aren't that different from geese after all…

Chapter 2
Birds of a Feather

Geese are intelligent birds. They don't focus on <u>what</u> they need for their journey. They focus on <u>who</u> they need; then everything else just falls into place – it happens naturally as a matter of course. Birds of a feather flock together.

Can you relate to this statement? Can you think of how it might apply in your life?

I once heard an expression that suggests we are, 'the average of the five people we spend the most time with.' If there is any truth to this statement, then it's important to spend time with the right people – with people who encourage you – people who give you energy – people who make you a better person.

These people should be your birds of a feather – they should be in your flock.

Have you ever seen a flock of geese fly together? They

fly in perfect harmony – almost effortlessly through the air. This is another reason why geese are so special. There are many birds that don't flock together – but those birds don't fly very far either, do they?

Geese don't fly alone – and they don't fly with just any old group of birds. Geese fly with geese. Geese fly farther when they fly with their birds of a feather. Recall that geese can fly nearly twice as far when they fly together.

Do you have geese in your flock? Are you going twice as far?

It's natural to find our 'birds of a feather'. When we find them, everything fits seamlessly together – almost effortlessly. Fly with people who motivate and spur you on, and encourage them. Then there's no limit to what you can do together. Geese can fly faster, higher, and farther when they are together.

So, who are your 'birds of a feather'?

Chapter 3
The Power of V

Why do geese fly in a V?

Scientifically, we now know that when geese fly in a 'V', they help each other. When geese fly in the quintessential flying V, they carve a V-shaped slipstream for the birds behind them, making it easier for them to fly together. Geese actually help each other when they fly together in a V. The 'V' is a marvelous formation, because it allows the whole to be greater than the sum of the parts. Whenever geese fly together, they help each other. Nobody taught them how to do it – it's just natural.

Do you fly in a V?

Do you recall the expression: "we are the average of the five people we spend the most time with?" Coincidentally, the number five is commonly expressed by the Roman Numeral V. In lending this perspective, it is obvious that the Power of V is beyond the individual. The power of V is in the collective. This can be a very instructive way of looking at the Power of V.

Who is in your 'V' formation?
Are they 'birds of a feather'?

In psychology, there is a concept known as 'flow'. Psychological flow is: *'the mental state of operation in which a person performing an activity is fully immersed in a feeling of energized focus, full involvement, and enjoyment in the process of the activity. In essence, flow is characterized by complete absorption in what one does, or completely focused motivation.'* Arguably, the power of V helps geese find that state of flow in flight. Your V should too.

The best performing groups in life all move together in the same direction; and by moving together, they help each other. With the power of V, geese naturally help each other first, and because they help each other, they also help themselves. This is so important that is worth repeating: by helping others, they help themselves.

Consider the V formation. When geese fly in a 'V', the geese in front cut a slipstream through the air for the geese behind them to take advantage of. The geese in front help by reducing the effort required by their fellow geese behind them. They help their fellow geese.

But geese do something more wonderful in the V – they rotate positions. When the geese in front of the 'V' are fatigued, they rotate to the back of the 'V', where they benefit from the very same help that they once provided. Another goose takes the lead, and the formation continues, because they take turns sharing the collective burden. This is why the V is so powerful. Individually, geese are more concerned with being 'part of the V' than 'leading the V' – and they fly much farther because of this.

The Power of V is one of nature's best examples of gestalt: the whole is greater than the sum of its parts. By helping each other, geese help themselves.

The Power of 'V' can be appreciated on a higher level: geese naturally <u>create</u> 'V' patterns. Geese find birds of a feather, and harness the power of V to work together and go places in life. The 'V' is just a simple pattern that allows geese to achieve more by working together – it creates a simple pattern that allows them to help each other. Geese create 'V' patterns on every journey in life. They naturally create the structures that they need in life to succeed. The best part is that it comes naturally. The beautiful patterns in life are natural.

What does your 'V' look like?

Chapter 4
Good for the Goose

What's good for the goose is good for the gander.

This expression describes the nature of reciprocity – a principle that we can learn from geese. Reciprocity in its purest form is best characterized by the Golden Rule. The Golden Rule implores us to: do unto others as you would have them do unto you. Geese are naturally empathetic creatures that embody the Golden Rule in so many ways.

One of the best examples of this is at the core of this teaching: geese honk. Geese honk to encourage each other. When one goose honks, the others reciprocate by joining in and encouraging each another. Geese give each other exactly what they need at any given moment. Empathy is part of their nature. That's part of what makes geese such amazing creatures.

Recall that when geese are in the 'V' formation, that they rotate positions – they help each other by literally taking their place – by sharing a collective burden to accomplish something greater than any individual could. Geese help each other all of the time in everything they do – they work as a collective. How often do you place yourself in someone else's shoes?

Geese go one step further. If a goose is wounded in flight and breaks the 'V' formation, it is very common for two or three other geese to break away from the V, and tend to the injured goose until it can continue its journey. Geese help each other before they help themselves. Think about that: geese *naturally* help each other before they help themselves. Isn't that a wonderful way to be?

It is no coincidence that geese accomplish an amazing journey every single year, and at the same time, express empathy the whole way. These things are connected. Where would you go this year if your birds of a feather constantly encouraged you, took your place whenever you asked, and followed you in your time of need? What could possibly stop you then?

Express empathy and it will naturally be returned to you.

Wherever you might be on your journey, take a moment to consider how you can apply the Golden Rule in your life. How can you treat others as you would like to be treated? Where are the opportunities for you to encourage others? What can you do to help others before you help yourself?

Act like geese do. Express your natural kindness. Be empathetic. Geese do it all of the time.

After all, if it's good for the goose, it's good for the gander...

Chapter 5
Simple Patterns, Repeated

Geese exhibit many patterns. It's important to understand the importance of these patterns, and it is equally important to understand how they fit together. Geese build so many patterns in their lives, that they build patterns of patterns. It's helpful to think of these patterns as different 'layers' of patterns – kind of like the layers of an onion. The simple patterns in the centre allow greater patterns to grow on the outside.

Simple patterns in and of themselves are extremely important, but it is just as important to understand how the simple patterns in life connect *together*. We started our journey together with the most basic pattern that enables any goose to achieve more than other birds: honking. Like the layers of the onion, this 'core' pattern of honking allows geese to find birds of a feather, create 'V' formations, share empathy, and complete an incredible journey every year. They are all built from the same principle… Simple patterns, repeated.

What are the simple patterns, repeated, that have helped you grow in life? What structures help you succeed? Can you identify recurring 'patterns' that connect in your past? I would encourage you to spend a few minutes now to reach into your past, and think about the patterns in your life, and how they connect. How do simple patterns combine together to make you the special person that you are today?

I was once told that there is only one difference between most people and Olympic athletes. That difference is usually one simple pattern, repeated. It is usually just *one* pattern! Imagine how much we could achieve if we could have more than one simple pattern – if we had simple <u>patterns</u> repeated in our lives! What if we could simply choose new simple patterns, repeated, that would prepare us perfectly for our future? It seems quite simple – perhaps it is.

Geese are very clever birds. They already know which simple patterns they need in their lives – it comes naturally to them. Can you imagine how geese feel halfway along that incredible journey – when their muscles are aching, and they just want to give up? No matter how difficult that journey is; geese know exactly what they need in life at every moment, because they are focused on the journey, not the destination. That's why geese honk.

Think about the journey in your life, not the destination. What simple patterns, repeated, do you need <u>right now</u> for your journey?

Time is nothing more than simple patterns, repeated. Days turn into weeks, weeks into months, months into years, and so on. They are all connected. When you think of the simple patterns that will shape your life, remember why geese honk. A simple pattern that you repeat every day will be much more powerful than a simple pattern that you repeat once every year, or one that is not repeated at all.

Why not take a moment right now to write down a simple pattern that you would like to repeat every single day? If you find this difficult, then write down something that you want to improve. Better yet, do this activity with one of your 'birds of a feather' as a joint exercise. Then simply spend a few minutes on it every day – turn it into a simple pattern, repeated.

Remember, geese achieve something amazing every single year.

But they honk every single day...

Chapter 6
Preen your Wings

Geese have wings. People have talents. Fundamentally, these are the same thing – they are our natural gifts that help us go places in life. In a sense, they carry us through life. Every goose has wings, and every person has talents. It's time to understand and appreciate them.

Geese grow their wings. Geese don't spend their lives trying to grow new wings. They trust the wings that they were born with. They rely on their natural strengths – their natural abilities. This is an important lesson: our natural strengths help us go places.

As an exercise, write down all of the strengths that you have – every single strength you can think of. Then, take a few moments to group them – to refine them. Refer to the simple patterns that you identified in your life to find the common thread between them. Distil this list of strengths over and over again until you have only two words that really resonate with you – two words that define your two most powerful natural abilities – two words that embody your talents – two words that describe your essence. What are these two defining talents in your life? Write them down.

Name them.

These are your wings – these will help you fly.

Now that you understand your talents, appreciate them. We can learn a lot from geese. When geese aren't flying, they are often spending time preening their feathers – preening their wings. Geese can preen their feathers several times a day, sometimes for several hours. When geese preen their feathers, they align them and refine them for easier flight. When geese preen their feathers, they essentially pause to 'sharpen their tools' to help them go places in life.

Geese preen their wings – sometimes every day. How often do you preen yours?

Name your wings, and preen them. They will help you go places in life.

Chapter 7
Look Forward

There is a wonderful metaphor in "look forward", because as a statement, it is instructive on a number of levels: physical, mental, and emotional. I believe that geese "look forward" on all of these levels.

First, "look forward" has a physical connotation that suggests that we physically look forward to see what is ahead. To 'look forward' is to see farther. Geese do this all of the time; they always look forward when they are flying.

This is important, because it helps us understand what geese do not do – which is just as important as what they do. What we do in life is just as important as what we do not do in life.

If you have ever watched geese fly, you will notice that they look forward – and in a group, geese look forward in the same direction. What you might not notice, and this is equally important, is that geese never look backward.

When geese fly, they don't look back. They don't look at what they are giving up, or what they are leaving behind. They look forward. Geese can't fly very far if they look backward.

Think about it: have you ever seen geese fly with their heads looking backwards?

Geese don't fly looking backward – geese fly looking forward. That's how they get to wherever they want to go. This frames why it is so important to 'look forward', just like geese do. Chin up, look forward.

Let's take this statement to the next level. To 'look forward' can also be a mental instruction through time – it can also mean, 'see the future', or 'imagine the future'. This is a very powerful statement. The future is a wonderful concept, because we can create it in our imagination. We can start to change the future just by thinking about it. The future offers boundless possibilities, limited only by our imagination.

In the mental context, when we 'look forward', we see where we want to go. When we see the future that we want, we bring ourselves closer to it. Our focus creates our reality. Great inventors, great athletes, and great birds all understand this. This applies to geese too: their focus creates their reality.

Take a few moments to look forward right now. What do you want your future look like?

"Look forward" also has an emotional application. When we 'look forward' to something, we are in joyful anticipation of it. In the emotional context, to "look forward" instructs us to be positive – to be enthused. This is the most important aspect in looking forward, because a positive mindset can influence and shape both the physical and mental states of 'look forward'.

What if we could change how we feel, so that we 'look forward' to everything? Imagine how great life would be if we could have the power of positivity within us all of the time. Geese have it.

Remember that geese honk throughout their entire journey, regardless of whether or not the sun is shining. Their positivity - their encouragement, is not just reserved for the destination – it is present throughout the entire journey, regardless of the circumstances. There are many birds that let their environment dictate their behaviour. Geese don't let their environment dictate their emotions. Geese let their emotions determine their environment.

If we can "look forward" in all three contexts – if we can control our physical, mental, and emotional states to 'look forward', then we can shape our future. Geese do it.

So what are you waiting for? Look forward.

🐦 🦆 🐦

Chapter 8
Stick your Neck out

If a goose wants to fly – if it wants to go places in life, it first has to stick its neck out.

Geese take risks in life. Every year, geese leave their home. They leave everything they know behind. They embark on a long, often dangerous journey into the unknown. Geese trust their natural abilities in life – for food, for shelter, for transport, for companionship – for everything. Do you trust your natural abilities for everything that you need?

You can decide where to fly in life, how high, and with whom. Don't be afraid of leaving something behind. Geese leave everything behind every single year. They even leave their own home. If it's not there when they get back, they find a new home. We can learn a lot from geese. Geese don't need "stuff" to go places in life. Geese only need each other.

What do you think? Is the question: *What* do you need

to go places in life? Or is the question: *Who* do you need to go places in life?

Recall that geese look forward – they don't look backward – they don't focus on what they might lose, or what they leave behind. Geese have a natural propensity to move forward in life, to take risks, and to trust their birds of a feather. Geese trust their natural abilities – they trust their talents.

How do you 'stick your neck out' in life? What do you need to let go of? What risks do you need to take in order to grow? What do you need to give up in order to go up?

Geese grow every single year by flying out of their comfort zone – they fly away from what is familiar. Geese challenge themselves in new environments because they stick their neck out every year. A goose can only fly if it sticks its neck out.

How can you grow by flying out of your comfort zone? How can you extend yourself, and push your limits?

Remember: if you want to fly, you have to stick your neck out…

Chapter 9
Fly

Geese are wonderful creatures.

Most birds accept the weather – good and bad. Their natural instincts help them survive whatever conditions pass. Most birds adapt. Geese are a bit different though, aren't they? Geese don't accept bad weather – it isn't in their nature. Geese find good weather. Geese *make* good weather.

Geese fly.

Whether they realise it or not, geese create their own world – they choose their own environment. Whenever geese want new scenery, they change it. They simply fly away. It is natural for geese to move on. How do you change the scenery in your life? How do you *'make good weather'* in your life?

Whether we acknowledge it or not, we create our own world – we choose our own environment. Just as we choose our 'birds of a feather', we also choose our own surroundings. We decide who we want to spend our time with, and where we want to spend it. Even more importantly, we choose *how* we spend our time; whether or not we enjoy ourselves in any situation, good or bad, is completely up to us.

In other words, we choose our own flight path in life. As the expression goes, 'Our attitude determines our altitude'.

Geese fly wherever they want to go. They ultimately choose where they want to be. They rely on their natural instincts in life to go places, and their natural abilities to get there. Sometimes, geese have to fly through a big storm or two to get where they are going. But geese still fly, and even in the middle of a storm, geese honk. Whenever you feel like you are going through a storm in life, remember everything you can about geese. Remember why geese honk.

If you don't like the environment in your life, change it. Rely on your natural abilities – rely on your talents to create your environment. Trust your wings, look forward, stick your neck out, and fly.

When geese fly, they move much faster than when they are grounded – they can really go places. Geese move faster when they fly – they create new places in life. You can too.

Use your wings.
Make your own good weather.
Fly.

Chapter 10
3,000 Feet

Geese fly at 3,000 feet.

When geese are on the ground, they can only see so far; they can only look forward so far. But when geese fly, they can look forward much farther; they can see almost everything.

At 3,000 feet, geese gain perspective.

Imagine how much farther geese can see when they are flying at 3,000 feet. What if you could view your life from 3,000 feet – what would you see? What would really be important in life? How would your 'simple patterns, repeated' connect together? What would your journey look like? What <u>could</u> your journey look like?

Think about your life from 3,000 feet. What new observations come into focus?

Have you ever watched a conversation from 3,000 feet?

When you 'level up' in a conversation, you can see much more. At 3,000 feet, you can uncover the emotional layers, the thought patterns, and conversational dynamics that create the essence of any interaction. These things can't be seen when you are grounded in the conversation.

Have you ever looked at your problems from 3,000 feet? When you bring yourself above a problem, you are able to see past the problem – you can see solutions. You are able to see what is important – what is really meaningful. You are able to see the big picture. It's much easier to solve a problem when you move up, and take yourself out of it.

Have you ever looked at yourself from 3,000 feet? What do you look like from 3,000 feet? How do you feel most of the time? How often do you honk? What are your most common behaviours? Who do you look like?

When we think and act from 3,000 feet, we level up in life – we see more of our world. We allow ourselves to grow.

View your world from 3,000 feet: it is far better than being grounded…

Notes

Randy Gadient

Randy Gadient

Contents

CHAPTER ONE

Architecture of India

The <u>Taj Mahal</u>, the most famous building depicting the <u>Mughal architecture</u>in India.

The <u>Lakshmana Temple, Khajuraho</u>, in the northern style of <u>Hindu temple architecture</u>, 10th century.

The **architecture of India**is rooted in its <u>history</u>, <u>culture</u>and <u>religion</u>. Among a number of architectural styles and traditions, the contrasting <u>Hindu temple architecture</u>and <u>Indo-Islamic architecture</u>are the best known historical styles. Both of these, but especially the former, have a number of regional styles within them. An early example of town planning was the Harappan architecture of the Indus Valley Civilisation. People lived in cities with baked brick houses, streets in a grid layout, elaborate drainage systems, water supply systems, granaries, citadels, and clusters of large non-residential buildings. Much other early Indian architecture was in wood, which has not survived.

Hindu temple architecture is mainly divided into <u>Dravidian</u>and <u>Nagara</u>styles. Dravidian architecture flourished during the rule of the <u>Chola</u>, <u>Chera</u>, and <u>Pandyan</u>empires, as well as the <u>Vijayanagara Empire</u>.

The first major <u>Islamic</u>kingdom in India was the <u>Delhi Sultanate</u>, which led to the development of <u>Indo-Islamic architecture</u>, combining Indian and Islamic features. The rule of the <u>Mughal Empire</u>, when <u>Mughal</u>

architectureevolved, is regarded as the zenith of Indo-Islamic architecture, with the Taj Mahalbeing the high point of their contribution. Indo-Islamic architecture influenced the Rajputand Sikhstyles as well.

During the British colonial period, European styles including neoclassical, gothic revival, and baroquebecame prevalent across India. The amalgamation of Indo-Islamic and European styles led to a new style, known as the Indo-Saracenicstyle. After independence, modernist ideas spread among Indian architects as a way of progressing from the colonial culture. Le Corbusier, who designed the city of Chandigarhinfluenced a generation of architects towards modernism in the 20th century. The economic reforms of 1991further bolstered the urban architecture of India as the country became more integrated with the world's economy. Traditional *Vastu Shastra* remains influential in India's architecture during the contemporary era.[1]

Contents

Indus Valley Civilization (2600 BCE – 1900 BCE)[edit]
Main articles: Ancient Indian architectureand Harappan architecture

The ruins of Dholavira

The Indus Valley Civilizationcovered a large area around the Indus Riverbasin and beyond in late Bronze Age India. In its mature phase, from about 2600 to 1900 BCE, it produced several cities marked by great uniformity within and between sites, including Harappa, Lothal, and the

UNESCO World Heritage SiteMohenjo-daro. The civic and town planningand engineering aspects of these are remarkable, but the design of the buildings is "of a startling utilitarian character". There are granaries, drains, water-courses and tanks, but neither palaces nor temples have been identified, though cities have a central raised and fortified "citadel".[2]Mohenjo-daro has wells which may be the predecessors of the stepwell.[3]As many as 700 wells have been discovered in just one section of the city, leading scholars to believe that 'cylindrical brick lined wells' were invented by the Indus Valley Civilization.[3]

Architectural decoration is extremely minimal, though there are "narrow pointed niches" inside some buildings. Most of the art found is in miniature forms like seals, and mainly in terracotta, but there are very few larger sculptures of figures. In most sites fired mud-brick (not sun-baked as in Mesopotamia) is used exclusively as the building material, but a few such as Dholaviraare in stone. Most houses have two storeys, and very uniform sizes and plans. The large cities declined relatively quickly, for unknown reasons, leaving a less sophisticated village culture behind.[4]

600 BCE—250 CE

Further information: Ancient Indian architecture, Buddhist architecture, and Indian rock-cut architecture

Conjectural reconstruction of the main gate of Kushinagarcirca 500 BCE adapted from a relief at Sanchi.

City of Kushinagar in the 5th century BCE according to a 1st century BCE frieze in Sanchi Stupa 1 Southern Gate.

After the Indus Valley Civilization, there are few traces of Indian architecture, which probably mostly used wood, or brick which has been recycled, until around the time of the Maurya Empire, from 322 to 185 BCE. From this period for several centuries onwards, much the best remains are of Indian rock-cut architecture, mostly Buddhist, and there are also a number of Buddhist images that give very useful information.

Buddhist construction of monastic buildings apparently begins before the death of Buddha, probably around 400 BCE.[5]This first generation only survives in floor-plans, notably at the Jivakarama viharain Bihar.

Walled and moated cities with large gates and multi-storied buildings which consistently used chaityaarches, no doubt in wood, for roofs and upper structures above more solid storeys are important features of the architecture during this period. The reliefs of Sanchi, dated to the 1st centuries BCE-CE, show cities such as Kushinagaror Rajagrihaas splendid walled cities, as in the *Royal cortege leaving Rajagriha*or *War over the Buddha's relics*. These views of ancient Indian cities have been relied on for the understanding of ancient Indian urban architecture.[6]

In the case of the Mauryan capital Pataliputra(near Patna), we have Greek accounts, and that of Faxian; Megasthenes(a visitor around 300 BCE) mentions 564 towers and 64 gates in the city walls. Modern excavations have uncovered a "massive palisade of teak beams held together with iron dowels".[7]A huge *apadana*-like hall with eighty sandstone columns shows clear influence from contemporary AchaemenidPersia.[8]The single massive sandstone Pataliputra capitalshows clear Hellenisticfeatures, reaching India via Persia.[9]The famous Ashoka columnsshow great sophistication, and a variety of influences in their details. In both these cases a now-vanished Indian predecessor tradition in wood is likely.[10]

Post-Maha-Janapadas Architecture

•

The Great Stupa at <u>Sanchi</u>(4th–1st century BCE). The dome-shaped stupa was used in India as a commemorative monument associated with storing sacred relics.

•

Illustration of the stupa built by Asoka at <u>Bodh Gaya</u>, on the location of the later <u>Mahabodhi Temple</u>. Sculpture of the <u>Satavahana</u>period at <u>Sanchi</u>, 1st century CE

Such a tradition is extremely clear in the case of the earliest-known examples of <u>rock-cut architecture</u>, the state-sponsored <u>Barabar caves</u>in <u>Bihar</u>, personally dedicated by <u>Ashoka</u>circa 250 BCE. The entrance of the <u>Lomas Rishi Cave</u>there has a sculpted doorway that clearly copies a wooden style in stone, which is a recurrent feature of rock-cut caves for some time. These artificial caves exhibit an amazing level of technical proficiency, the extremely hard <u>granite</u>rock being cut in geometrical fashion and given the <u>Mauryan polish</u>, also found on sculpture.[11][12]Later rock-cut <u>viharas</u>, occupied by monastic communities, survive, mostly in Western India, and in <u>Bengal</u>the floor-plans of brick-built equivalents survive. The elaborately decorated facades and "chaitya halls" of many rock-cut sites are believed to reflect vanished free-standing buildings elsewhere.

The Buddhist stupa, a dome shaped monument, was used in India as a commemorative monument associated with storing sacred relics.[13]The stupa architecture was adopted in Southeastand East Asia, where it became prominent as a Buddhistmonument used for enshrining sacred relics.[13]Guard rails—consisting of posts, crossbars, and a coping—became a feature of safety surrounding a stupa.[14]Temples—build on elliptical, circular, quadrilateral, or apsidal plans—were constructed using brick and timber.[14]The Indian gateway arches, the *torana*, reached East Asia with the spread of Buddhism.[15]Some scholars hold that *torii* derives from the torana gates at the Buddhist historic site of Sanchi(3rd century BCE – 11th century CE).[16]

Rock-cut stepwellsin India date from 200–400 CE.[17]Subsequently, the construction of wells at Dhank (550–625 CE) and stepped ponds at Bhinmal(850–950 CE) took place.[17]Cave temples became prominent throughout western India, incorporating various unique features to give rise to cave architecture in places such as Ajantaand Ellora.[14]

A very important development, the emergence of the shikaraor temple tower, is today best evidenced by the Buddhist Mahabodhi Temple. This was already several centuries old when the first very vertical structure replaced an Ashokan original, apparently around 150-200 CE. The current brick-built tower, probably a good deal larger, dates to the Guptaperiod, in the 5th or 6th centuries.[18]

Gupta architecture

Dashavatara Temple, Deogarhis a Vishnu Hindu temple built during the early 6th century, near the end of the Gupta period.

For reasons that are not entirely clear, for the most part the Gupta period represented a hiatus in Indian rock-cut architecture, with the first wave of construction finishing before the empire was assembled, and the second wave beginning in the late 5th century, after it ended. This is the case, for example, at the Ajanta Caves, with an early group made by 220 CE at the latest, and a later one probably all after about 460.[19]Instead, the period has left almost the first surviving free-standing structures in India, in particular, the beginnings of Hindu temple architecture. As Milo Beachputs it: "Under the Guptas, India was quick to join the rest of the medieval world in a passion for housing precious objects in stylized architectural frameworks",[20]the "precious objects" being primarily the icons of gods.

The most famous remaining monuments in a broadly Gupta style, the caves at Ajanta, Elephanta, and Ellora(respectively Buddhist, Hindu, and mixed including Jain) were in fact produced under other dynasties in Central India, and in the case of Ellora after the Gupta period, but primarily reflect the monumentality and balance of Guptan style. Ajanta contains by far the most significant survivals of painting from this and the surrounding periods, showing a mature form which had probably had a long development, mainly in painting palaces.[21]The Hindu Udayagiri Cavesactually record connections with the dynasty and its ministers,[22]and the Dashavatara Templeat Deogarhis a major temple, one of the earliest to survive, with important sculpture.[23]

Examples of early North Indian Hindu temples that have survived after the Udayagiri Cavesin Madhya Pradeshinclude those at Tigawa(early 5th century),[24]SanchiTemple 17 (similar, but respectively Hindu and Buddhist), Deogarh, Parvati Temple, Nachna(465),[25]Bhitargaon, the largest Gupta brick temple to survive,[26]and Lakshman Brick Temple, Sirpur(600–625 CE). Gop Templein Gujarat(c. 550 or later) is an oddity, with no surviving close comparator.[27]

There are a number of different broad models, which would continue to be the case for more than a century after the Gupta period, but temples such as Tigawa and Sanchi Temple 17, which are small but massively built stone prostylebuildings with a sanctuary and a columned porch, show the most common basic plan that continues today. Both of these have flat roofs over the sanctuary, which would become uncommon by about the 8th century. The Mahabodhi Temple, Bhitargaon, Deogarh and Gop already all show high superstructures of different shapes.[28]The Chejarla Kapoteswara templedemonstrates that free-standing chaitya-hall temples with barrel roofs continued to be built, probably with many smaller examples in wood.[29]

•

A tetrastyleprostyleGupta periodtemple at Sanchibesides the Apsidal hall with Mauryafoundation, an example of Buddhist architecture. 5th century CE.

•

The Hindu TigawaTemple, early 5th century.

•

The current structure of the Mahabodhi Templedates to the Gupta era, 5th century CE. Marking the location where the Buddha is said to have attained enlightenment.

•

Vishnu temple in Eran, 5th-6th century.

•

The Buddhaguptapillar at Eran (c.476–495 CE).
Temple architecture
Main article: Hindu temple architecture

The rock-cut Shore Templeof the temples in Mahabalipuram, Tamil Nadu, 700–728. Showing the typical _dravida_form of tower.

The basic elements of the Hindu temple remain the same across all periods and styles. The most essential feature is the inner sanctuary, the _garbha griha_ or womb-chamber, where the primary _Murti_ or cult image of a deity is housed in a simple bare cell. Around this chamber there are often other structures and buildings, in the largest cases covering several acres. On the exterior, the garbhagriha is crowned by a tower-like _shikhara_, also called the _vimana_ in the south.[30] The shrine building may include an ambulatory for _parikrama_ (circumambulation), one or more mandapas or congregation halls, and sometimes an antarala antechamber and porch between garbhagriha and mandapa. There may be further shrines or other buildings, connected or detached, in large temples, together with other small temples in the compound.[31] The whole temple compound is usually enclosed by a wall, and the temple itself, or sometimes the whole compound, is often raised on a plinth(_adhiṣṭhāna_). Large areas of the structure are often decorated with carving, including figurative images of deities and other religious figures. Beyond these basic but crucial similarities, the visible stylistic forms of the temple vary greatly and have a very complicated development.[32]

By about the 7th century CE most main features of the Hindu temple were established along with theoretical texts on temple architecture and building methods.[33] Already three styles of temple were identified in these: _nagara_, _dravida_ and _vesara_, though these were not yet associated with regions of India, and the original meanings may not fully align with modern uses of the terms.[32] In Karnataka, the group of 7th and 8th-century temples at Pattadakal famously mixes forms later associated with both north and south,[34] as does that at Aihole, which still includes apsidalchaitya hall-type plans.[35]

For most modern writers, *nagara* refers to north Indian styles, most easily recognised by a high and curving *shikhara* over the sanctuary, *dravida* or Dravidian architecture is the broad South Indian style, where the superstructure over the sanctuary is not usually extremely high, and has a straight profile, rising in series of terraces to form a sort of decorated pyramid (today often dwarfed in larger temples by the far larger gopuram outer gateways, a much later development).[36] The ancient term vesara is also used by some modern writers, to describe a temple style with characteristics of both the northern and southern traditions. These come from the Deccan and other fairly central parts of India. There is some disagreement among those who use the term, as to the exact period and styles it represents, and other writers prefer to avoid it; temples some describe as vesara are mostly assigned to the northern tradition by those, but are regarded as a kind of northern *dravida* by others.[37]

Early

Kailasa temple, Ellora, the largest rock-cut Hindu temple.[38]

There are hardly any remains of Hindu temples before the Gupta dynastyin the 4th century CE; no doubt there were earlier structures in timber-based architecture. The rock-cutUdayagiri Cavesare among the most important early sites.[39]The earliest preserved Hindu temples are simple cell-like stone temples, some rock-cut and others structural, as at Sanchi.[40]By the 6th or 7th century, these evolved into high shikharastone superstructures. However, there is inscriptional evidence such as the ancient Gangadhara inscription from about 424 CE, states Meister, that towering temples existed before this time and these were possibly made from more perishable material. These temples have not survived.[40][25]

Examples of early major North Indian temples that have survived after the Udayagiri Cavesin Madhya Pradeshinclude Deogarh, Parvati Temple, Nachna(465 CE),[25]Lalitpur District(c. 525 CE), Lakshman Brick Temple, Sirpur(600-625 CE); Rajiv Lochan temple, Rajim(7th-century CE).[41]

No pre-7th century CE South Indian style stone temples have survived. Examples of early major South Indian temples that have survived, some in ruins, include the diverse styles at Mahabalipuram, from the 7th and 8th centuries. However, according to Meister, the Mahabalipuram temples are "monolithic models of a variety of formal structures all of which already can be said to typify a developed "Dravida" (South Indian) order". They suggest a tradition and a knowledge base existed in South India by the time of the early Chalukya and Pallava era when these were built. Other examples are found in Aiholeand Pattadakal.[41][42]

From between about the 7th and 13th centuries a large number of temples and their ruins have survived (though far fewer than once existed). Many regional styles developed, very often following political divisions, as large temples were typically built with royal patronage. In the north, Muslim invasionsfrom the 11th century onwards reduced the building of temples, and saw the loss of many existing ones.[33]The south also witnessed Hindu-Muslim conflict that affected the temples, but the region was relatively less affected than the north.[43]In late 14th century, the Hindu Vijayanagara Empirecame to power and controlled much of South India. During this period, the distinctive very tall gopuramgatehouse actually a late development, from the 12th century or later, typically added to older large temples.[33]

The South Indian temple consists essentially of a square-chambered sanctuary topped by a superstructure, tower, or spire and an attached pillared porch or hall (maṇḍapa or maṇṭapam), enclosed by a peristyle of cells within a rectangular court. The external walls of the temple are segmented by pilasters and carry niches housing sculpture. The superstructure or tower above the sanctuary is of the kūṭina type and consists of an arrangement of gradually receding stories in a pyramidal shape. Each story is delineated by a parapet of miniature shrines, square at the corners and rectangular with barrel-vault roofs at the centre.

Later[edit]

Examples of Hindu Architecture throughout India

North Indiantemples showed increased elevation of the wall and elaborate spire by the 10th century.[44]On the shikara, the oldest form, called *latina*, with wide shallow projections running up the sides, developed alternative forms with many smaller "spirelets" (*urushringa*). Two varieties of these are called *sekhari*, where the sub-spires extend vertically, and *bhumija*, where individual sub-spires are arrayed in rows and columns.

Richly decorated temples—including the complex at Khajuraho—were constructed in Central India.[44]Examples include the Lingaraj Templeat Bhubaneshwarin Odisha, Sun Templeat Konarkin Odisha, Brihadeeswarar Templeat Thanjavurin Tamil Nadu. Indian traders brought Indian architecture to South east Asiathrough various trade routes.[45]

Styles called *vesara* include the early Badami Chalukya Architecture, Western Chalukya architecture, and finally Hoysala architecture. Other regional styles include those of Bengal, Kashmirand other Himalayan areas, Karnataka, Kalinga architecture, and Māru-Gurjara architecture.

Sculptures at the Hoysaleswara Templeat Halebidu.

Hoysala architectureis the distinctive building style developed under the rule of the Hoysala Empirein the region historically known as *Karnata*, today's Karnataka, India, between the 11th and the 14th centuries.[46]Large and small temples built during this era remain as examples of the Hoysala architectural style, including the Chennakesava Templeat Belur, the Hoysaleswara Templeat Halebidu, and the Kesava Templeat Somanathapura. Other examples of fine Hoysala craftmanship are the temples at Belavadi, Amrithapura, and Nuggehalli. Study of the Hoysala architectural style has revealed a negligible Indo-Aryan influence while the impact of Southern Indian style is more distinct.[47]A feature of Hoysala temple architecture is its attention to detail and skilled craftsmanship. The temples of Belur and Halebidu are proposed UNESCOworld heritage sites.[48]Approximately 100 Hoysala temples survive today.[49]

Vijayanagara architecture of the period (1336–1565 CE) was a notable building style evolved by the Vijayanagar empire that ruled most of South India from their capital at Vijayanagara on the banks of the Tungabhadra River in present-day Karnataka.[50] The architecture of the temples built during the reign of the Vijayanagara empire had elements of political authority.[51] This resulted in the creation of a distinctive imperial style of architecture which featured prominently not only in temples but also in administrative structures across the deccan.[52] The Vijayanagara style is a combination of the Chalukya, Hoysala, Pandya and Chola styles which evolved earlier in the centuries when these empires ruled and is characterised by a return to the simplistic and serene art of the past.[53]

The Warangal Fort, Thousand Pillar Temple, and Ramappa Temple are examples of Kakatiya architecture.[54]

Jain architecture

Palitana Jain Temples

Jain Temple complex, Deogarh, Uttar Pradesh, before 862

Main article: Jain temple

Jain temple architecture is generally close to Hindu temple architecture, and in ancient times Buddhist religious architecture. Normally the same builders and carvers worked for all religions, and regional and period styles are generally similar. The basic layout of a Hindu and most Jain temples has consisted of a small garbhagriha or sanctuary for the main murti or cult images, over which the high superstructure rises, then one or more larger mandapa halls.

The earliest survivals of Jain architecture are part of the Indian rock-cut architecturetradition, initially shared with Buddhism, and by the end of the classical period with Hinduism. Very often numbers of rock-cut Jain temples and monasteries share a site with those of the other religions, as at Udayagiri, Bava Pyara, Ellora, Aihole, Badami, and Kalugumalai. The Ellora Cavesare a late site, which contains temples of all three religions, as the earlier Buddhist ones give way to later Hindu excavations.

There is considerable similarity between the styles of the different religions, but often the Jains placed large figures of one or more of the 24 tirthankarasin the open air rather than inside the shrine. These statues later began to be very large, normally standing nude figures in the *kayotsarga* meditation position (which is similar to standing at attention). Examples include the Gopachal rock cut Jain monumentsand the Siddhachal Caves, with groups of statues, and a number of single figures including the 12th-century Gommateshwara statue, and the modern Statue of Vasupujyaand, largest of all at 108 feet (32.9 meters) tall, the Statue of Ahimsa.

Regional differences in Hindu temples are largely reflected in Jain ones, except that Māru-Gurjara architectureor the "Solanki style" has become to some extent a pan-Indian, indeed pan-global Jain style. This is a particular temple style from Gujaratand Rajasthan(both regions with a strong Jain presence) that originated in both Hindu and Jain temples around 1000, but became enduringly popular with Jain patrons, spreading to other parts of India and the global Jain diasporaof the last century. It has remained in use, in somewhat modified form, to the present day, indeed also becoming popular again for some Hindu temples in the last century. The style is seen in the groups of pilgrimage temples at <u>Dilwara</u>on <u>Mount Abu</u>, <u>Taranga</u>, <u>Girnar</u>and <u>Palitana</u>.[55]

The main buildings of the largest Dilwara temples are surrounded by "cloister" screens of *devakulikā* shrines, and are fairly plain on the outer walls of these; in the case of the Vimal Vasahi this screen was a later addition, around the time of the second temple.[56]Surrounding the main temple with a curtain of shrines was to become a distinctive feature of the Jain temples of West India, still employed in some modern temples.[57]

Mostly funded by private individuals or groups, and catering to a smaller population, Jain temples tend to be at the small or middle end of the range of sizes, but at pilgrimage sites they may cluster in large groups - there are altogether several hundred at Palitana, tightly packed within several high-walled compounds called "tuks" or "tonks".[58]Temple charitable trusts, such as the very large <u>Anandji Kalyanji Trust</u>, founded in the 17th century and now maintaining 1,200 temples, play a very important role in funding temple building and maintenance.

Indo-Islamic architecture

The <u>Charminar</u>, built in the 16th century by the <u>Golconda Sultanate</u>.

Main article: <u>Indo-Islamic architecture</u>

Early[edit]

The earliest examples of <u>Indo-Islamic architecture</u>were constructed during this period by the <u>Delhi Sultanates</u>, most famously the <u>Qutb Minar complex</u>, which was designated a <u>UNESCO World Heritage Site</u>in 1993. The complex consists of <u>Qutb Minar</u>, a brick minaret commissioned by <u>Qutub-ud-Din Aibak</u>, as well as other monuments built by successive Delhi Sultans.[59]Alai Minar, a minaret twice the size of Qutb Minarwas commissioned by Alauddin Khiljibut never completed. Other examples include the Tughlaqabad Fortand Hauz Khas Complex.

Significant regional stylesdeveloped in the independent sultanates formed when the Tughlaq empire weakened in the mid-14th century, and lasted until most were absorbed into the Mughal Empire in the 16th century. Apart from the sultanates of the Deccan Plateau, Gujarat, Bengal, and Kashmir, the architecture of the Malwaand Jaunpur sultanatesalso left some significant buildings.[60]

Notable buildings of the Bahmaniand Deccan sultanatesin the Deccan include the Charminar, Mecca Masjid, Qutb Shahi Tombs, Madrasa Mahmud Gawanand Gol Gumbaz.[61][62]

The style of the Bengal Sultanatemostly used brick, with characteristic features being indigenous Bengali elements, such as curved roofs, corner towers and complex terracottaornamentation.[63]which were with blended . One feature in the sultanate was the relative absence of minarets.[64]Many small and medium-sized medieval mosques, with multiple domes and artistic nichemihrabs, were constructed throughout the region.[64]The largest mosque in the Indian subcontinent was the 14th century Adina Mosque. Built of stone demolished from temples, it featured a monumental ribbed barrel vault over the central nave, the first such giant vault used anywhere in the subcontinent. The mosque was modelled on the imperial Sasanianstyle of Persia.[65]The Sultanate style flourished between the 14th and 16th centuries. A provincial style influenced by North India evolved in Mughal Bengal during the 17th and 18th centuries. The Mughals also copied the Bengali do-chalaroof tradition for mausoleums in North

India.[66]

Mughal Empire[edit]

Main article: Mughal architecture

Humayun's Tomb, Delhi, the first fully developed Mughal imperial tomb, 1569–70 CE.[67]

The most famous Indo-Islamic style is Mughal architecture. Its most prominent examples are the series of imperial mausolea, which started with the pivotal Tomb of Humayun, but is best known for the Taj Mahal.

It is known for features including monumental buildings with large, bulbous onion domes, surrounded by gardens on all four sides, and delicate ornamentation work, including *pachin kari*decorative work and *jali*-latticed screens.

Red Fortwas the main residence of the Mughal emperorsfor nearly 200 years, until 1856.[68]

The Red Fortat Agra(1565–74) and the walled city of Fatehpur Sikri(1569–74)[69]are among the architectural achievements of this time—as is the Taj Mahal, built as a tomb for Queen Mumtaz Mahalby Shah Jahan(1628–58).[70]Employing the double dome, the recessed archway, the depiction of any animal or human—an essential part of the Indian tradition—was forbidden in places of worship under Islam. The Taj Mahal does contain tilework of plant ornaments.[1]The architectureduring the Mughal Period, with its rulers being of Turco-Mongol origin, has shown a notable blend of Indian style combined with the Islamic. Taj Mahal in Agra, India is one of the wonders of the world.[71]

Later regional styles

Rajput Architecture[edit]

Main article: Architecture of Rajasthan

The Mughalarchitecture and painting influenced indigenous Rajput styles of art and architecture.[72]Rajput Architecture represents different types of buildings, which may broadly be classed either as secular or religious. The secular buildings are of various scales. These include temples, forts, stepwells, gardens, and palaces. The forts were specially built for defense and military purposes due to the Islamic invasions.

Rajput Architecture continued well into the 20th and 21st centuries, as the rulers of the princely statesof British Indiacommissioned vast palaces and other buildings, such as the Albert Hall Museum, Lalgarh Palace, and Umaid Bhawan Palace. These usually incorporated European styles as well, a practice which eventually led to the Indo-Saracenic style

•

Ranakpur Jain temple

•

City Palace

•

Chittor Fort

- Amer Fortand Jaigarh Fort

Sikh Architecture[edit]
Main article: Sikh architecture

The Golden Temple in Amritsar.

Sikh architecture was also highly influenced by Mughal architecture, and spread with the Sikh religion. The Golden Temple in Amritsar and Hazur Sahib are examples.

Maratha Architecture

Shaniwarwada palace fort in Pune.

The Maratha Rule from 17th to 19th Centuries, emerged during decline of Mughal Empire, Prominent buildings such as Shaniwar Wada, Lal Mahal in Pune are few examples.

Bengal Architecture

Main article: Architecture of Bengal

The **architecture of Bengal**, which comprises the modern country of Bangladesh and the Indian states of West Bengal, Tripura, and Assam's Barak Valley, has a long and rich history, blending indigenous elements from the Indian subcontinent, with influences from different parts of the world. Bengali architecture includes ancient urban architecture, religious architecture, rural vernacular architecture, colonial townhouses and country houses, and modern urban styles.[73]

The bungalow style is a notable architectural export of Bengal. The corner towers of Bengali religious buildings were replicated in medieval Southeast Asia. Bengali curved roofs, suitable for the very heavy rains, were adopted into a distinct local style of Indo-Islamic architecture, and used decoratively elsewhere in north India in <u>Mughal architecture</u>.[74]

Bengal is not rich in good stone for building, and traditional Bengali architecture mostly uses brick and wood, often reflecting the styles of the wood, bamboo and thatch styles of local <u>vernacular architecture</u>for houses. Decorative carved or <u>moulded</u>plaques of <u>terracotta</u>(the same material as the brick) are a special feature. The brick is extremely durable and disused ancient buildings were often used as a convenient source of materials by local people, often being stripped to their foundations over the centuries.

•

<u>Rasmancha, Bishnupur</u>

•

Bishnupur cluster of temples

•

<u>Jorbangla (douchala style)</u>

•

<u>Dakshineswar Kali Temple</u>, Kolkata. It features the Navratna style of roof.

•

Madan Mohan Temple

European colonial architecture

As with the Mughals, under European colonial rule, architecture became an emblem of power, designed to endorse the occupying power. Numerous European countries invaded India and created architectural styles reflective of their ancestral and adopted homes. The European colonizers created architecture that symbolized their mission of conquest, dedicated to the state or religion.[75]

The British, French, Dutch and the Portuguese were the main European powers that colonized parts of India.[76][77]

British Colonial Era: 1757–1947

<u>Lutyens' Delhi</u>

The Viceroy's House (now <u>Rashtrapati Bhavan</u>) was built for the <u>Viceroy of India</u>. It now serves as the official residence of the <u>President of India</u>.

The War Memorial Arch (now India Gate) is a memorial to 70,000 soldiers of the British Indian Armywho died in the First World War

The Secretariat Buildingis located in the North Block.

The Council House, built for the Imperial Legislative Council, is now Sansad Bhawan, and houses the Parliament of India.
Lutyens' Delhi,designed by Edwin Lutyens, houses all key government buildings of India.

Britain's legacy in India remains among others in building and infrastructure. The major cities colonized during this period were Madras, Calcutta, Bombay, Delhi, Agra, Bankipore, Karachi, Nagpur, Bhopal and

Hyderabad,[78][77]which saw the rise of Indo-Saracenic Revival architecture.

Black Town described in 1855 as "the minor streets, occupied by the natives are numerous, irregular and of various dimensions. Many of them are extremely narrow and ill-ventilated ... a hallow square, the rooms opening into a courtyard in the centre."[79]Garden houses were originally used as weekend houses for recreational use by the upper class British. Nonetheless, the garden house became ideal a full-time dwelling, deserting the fort in the 19th Century.[80]

Mumbai, (then known as Bombay) has some of the most prominent examples of British colonial architecture. This included the gothic revival(Victoria terminus, University of Mumbai, Rajabai Clock Tower, High Court, BMC Building), Indo-Saracenic(Prince of Wales Museum, Gateway of India, Taj Mahal Palace Hotel) and art deco(Eros Cinema, New India Assurance Building).[81]

Calcutta – Madras and Calcutta were similarly bordered by water and division of Indian in the north and British in the south. An Englishwoman noted in 1750 "the banks of the river are as one may say absolutely studded with elegant mansions called here as at Madras, garden houses." Esplanade-row is fronts the fort with lined palaces.[82][83]Indian villages in these areas consisted of clay and straw houses which later transformed into the metropolis of brick and stone.[84]

•

Madras High Courtbuildings are a prime example of Indo-Saracenic architecture, designed by JW Brassington under the guidance of British architect Henry Irwin.

•

The Viceregal Lodge, now Rashtrapati Niwas, in Shimladesigned by Henry Irwinin the Jacobethanstyle and built in the late 19th century.

Indo-Saracenic[edit]

Further information: Indo-Saracenic Revival architecture

Indo-Saracenic architectureevolved by combining Indian architectural features with European styles. Vincent Eschand George Wittetwere pioneers in this style.

The Victoria Memorialin Calcutta is the most effective symbolism of British Empire, built as a monument in tribute to Queen Victoria's reign. The plan of the building consists of one large central part covered with a larger

dome. Colonnades separate the two chambers. Each corner holds a smaller dome and is floored with marble plinth. The memorial stands on 26 hectares of garden surrounded by reflective pools.[85]

-

Victoria Memorial is a famous example is Indo-sarasenic architecture.

-

Calcutta High Court

-

Prinsep Ghat

-

Marble Palace, Kolkata

-

Hazarduari Palace, Murshidabad

-

Indian Museum, Kolkata

-

National library of India, Kolkata

Neoclassical]

Examples of Neoclassicalarchitecture in India include British Residency(1798) and Falaknuma Palace(1893) in Hyderabad, St Andrews Churchin Madras (1821),[86]Raj Bhawan(1803) and Metcalfe Hall(1844) in Kolkata, and Bangalore Town Hall(1935) in Bangalore.

Art Deco[edit]

The Art Decomovement of the early 20th century quickly spread to large parts of the world. The Indian Institute of Architects, founded in Bombay in 1929, played a prominent role in propagating the movement. The New India Assurance Building, Eros Cinemaand buildings along the Marine Drivein Mumbai are prime examples.[81]

Other Colonial powers[edit]

The Portuguesehad colonized parts of India, including Goaand Mumbai. The Madh Fort, St. John the Baptist Church, and Castella de Aguadain Mumbai are remnants of Portuguese Colonial rule. The Churches and Convents of Goa, an ensemble of seven churches built by the Portuguese in Goa are a UNESCO World Heritage Site.[87]

Republic of India (1947 onwards

In recent times there has been a movement of population from rural areas to urban centres of industry, leading to price rise in property in various cities of India.[88]Urban housing in India balances space constrictions and is aimed to serve the working class.[89]Growing awareness of ecology has influenced architecture in India during modern times.[90]

Climate responsive architecture has long been a feature of India's architecture but has been losing its significance as of late.[91]Indian architecture reflects its various socio-cultural sensibilities which vary from region to region.[91]Certain areas are traditionally held to be belonging to women.[91]Villages in India have features such as courtyards, loggias, terraces and balconies.[89]Calico, chintz, and palampore—of Indian origin—highlight the assimilation of Indian textiles in global interior design.[92]Roshandans, which are skylights-cum-ventilators, are a common feature in Indian homes, especially in North India.[93][94]

At the time of independence in 1947, India had only about 300 trained architects in a population of what was then 330 million, and only one training institution, the Indian Institute of Architects. Thus the first generation of Indian architects were educated abroad.

Panorama of the Indian Institute of Management Ahmedabaddesigned by Louis Kahn, and completed in 1961.

Some early architects were traditionalists, such as Ganesh Deolalikar, whose design for the Supreme Courtimitated the Lutyens-Bakerbuildings down to the last detail, and B.R. Manickam, who designed the Vidhana Soudhain Bangalore reminiscent of Indo-Saracenic architecture.

In 1950, French architect Le Corbusier, a pioneer of modernist architecture, was commissioned by Jawaharlal Nehruto design the city of Chandigarh. His plan called for residential, commercial and industrial areas, along with parks and transportation infrastructure. In the middle was the capitol, a complex of three government buildings – the Palace of Assembly, the High Court, and the Secretariat.[95]He also designed the Sanskar Kendraat Ahmedabad. Corbusier inspired the next generation of architects in India to work with modern, rather than revivalist styles.[96]

Other prominent examples of modernist architecture in India include IIM Ahmedabadby Louis Kahn(1961), IIT Delhiby Jugal Kishore Chodhury(1961), IIT Kanpurby Achyut Kanvinde(1963), IIM Bangaloreby B. V. Doshi(1973), Lotus Templeby Fariborz Sahba(1986), and Jawahar Kala Kendra(1992) and Vidhan Bhawan Bhopal(1996) by Charles Correa.[96]

Skyscrapers built in the international styleare becoming increasingly common in cities. This includes The 42(2019) and The Imperial(2010) by Hafeez Contractor. Other projects of the 21st century include IIT Hyderabadby Christopher Benninger(2015).

Notable ongoing projects in India include the city of Amaravati, Kolkata Museum of Modern Art, Sardar Patel Stadium, World One, and Navi Mumbai Airport.

-

Palace of Assembly, a part of the Capitol Complexat Chandigarhdesigned by Le Corbusier.[95]

-

Deekshabhoomi Stupa in Nagpurwas completed in 1956.[97]

-

Lotus Temple in Delhi, completed in 1986.[96]

-

Golden Pagoda in Namsai, completed in 2010.

www.ingramcontent.com/pod-product-compliance
Lightning Source LLC
Chambersburg PA
CBHW071525180526
45171CB00002B/388